D0313823

To Cuzack - C.F.
To Zack and Luke - K.U.

# OXFORD
### UNIVERSITY PRESS

Great Clarendon Street, Oxford OX2 6DP

Oxford University Press is a department of the University of Oxford.
It furthers the University's objective of excellence in research, scholarship,
and education by publishing worldwide in

Oxford  New York

Auckland  Bangkok  Buenos Aires  Cape Town  Chennai
Dar es Salaam  Delhi  Hong Kong  Istanbul  Karachi  Kolkata
Kuala Lumpur  Madrid  Melbourne  Mexico City  Mumbai  Nairobi
São Paulo  Shanghai  Singapore  Taipei  Tokyo  Toronto

with an associated company in Berlin

Oxford is a registered trade mark of Oxford University Press
in the UK and in certain other countries

Text copyright © Kaye Umansky 1999
Illustrations copyright © Chris Fisher 1999

The moral rights of the author/artist have been asserted

Database right Oxford University Press (maker)

First published in 1999
Second edition 2002

All rights reserved. No part of this publication may be reproduced,
stored in a retrieval system, or transmitted, in any form or by any means,
without the prior permission in writing of Oxford University Press,
or as expressly permitted by law, or under terms agreed with the appropriate
reprographics rights organization. Enquiries concerning reproduction
outside the scope of the above should be sent to the Rights Department,
Oxford University Press, at the address above

You must not circulate this book in any other binding or cover
and you must impose this same condition on any acquirer

British Library Cataloguing in Publication Data available

ISBN 0-19-910995-8

1 3 5 7 9 10 8 6 4 2

Printed in China

| Northamptonshire Libraries & Information Service | |
| --- | --- |
| | |
| Peters | 23-Jul-03 |
| 821 | £4.99 |
| | |

# Nonsense Counting Rhymes

Poems *by* Kaye Umansky

*Illustrated by* Chris Fisher

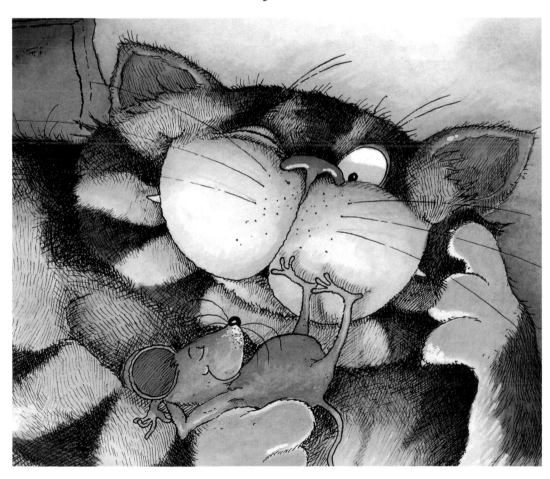

**OXFORD**

UNIVERSITY PRESS

# O
## Zero for Nero

Emperor Nero went fishing,
"I'm sure to get hundreds," said he.
But Emperor Nero caught zero,
And had to have pizza for tea.

# 1
# One Man Went to Mow

One man went to mow,
He couldn't work the mower,
He used a pair of scissors, so
The grass got cut much slower.

## 2
# Two Little Dicky Birds

Two little dicky birds
Playing in the trough.
Two little sticky birds
Got a telling off.
Go and clean your feathers!
Go and wash your wings!
Don't play in the trough again,
You mucky little things!

# 3
# Three Silly Goblins

Three silly goblins were painting a rose.

The first goblin painted the second one's nose.

The third one poured paint in the first goblin's shoe.

Were they good at the job? I don't think so, do you?

# 4
# Four Crazy Rabbits

Over my tail and whoops a daisy!
Four rabbits going crazy.
Here comes Farmer John.
Four rabbits going...going...gone!

# 5
# One, Two, Three, Four, Five

One, two, three, four, five,
Once I caught a shark alive,
Six, seven, eight, nine, ten,
Don't think I'll do that again!

# 6
# Sing a Song of Sixpence

Sing a song of sixpence,

A pocket full of cheese,

Four and twenty monkeys

Swinging in the trees.

They picked all the bananas

And dropped them on my head.

I had to call the monkey king

Who sent them off to bed.

# 7
# Seven Pirates

Shiver me timbers, set the sails,

Be sure to catch the breeze!

Seven pirates went a-sailing

On the seven salty seas.

The life was tough, the seas were rough,

They lasted seven years,

Then sailed home to their seven wives

Who gave them seven big cheers!

# 8
# Eight Cakes

Two, four, six, eight!

Count the cakes the giant ate.

Stop him quick! He'll eat the plate!

Oh dear. Too late.

# 9
# Nine Plump Pigeons

Three, six, nine! The day was fine.

Nine plump pigeons

Perching on the line.

The cat crept up, her jaws went snap!

And nine plump pigeons went

Flap, flap, flap!

# 10
# Ten Tubby Teddies

Ten tubby teddies on a trampoline,
Jump, teddy, jump! Jump, teddy, jump!
Their coats are red, their hats are green,
Jump, teddy, jump! Jump, teddy, jump!
They jumped so high, they were so keen,
Jump, teddy, jump! Jump, teddy, jump!
They made a hole in the trampoline,
Thump, teddy,

*thump,*

**thump,**

**THUMP!**

## If You Can't Sleep

"If you can't sleep, try counting sheep,

And soon you will be snoring."

That's what my mummy said to me,

But counting sheep was boring.

So I tried counting lions,

But the lions started *ROARING!*

I'm going back to sheep again.

Who said sheep were boring?

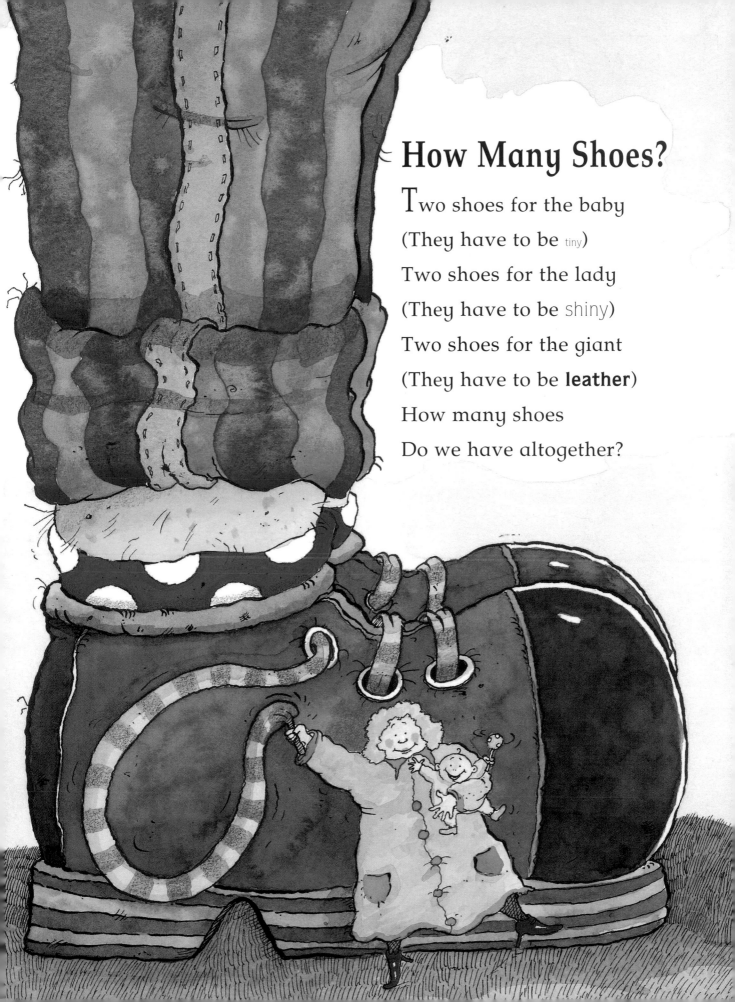

# How Many Shoes?

Two shoes for the baby
(They have to be tiny)
Two shoes for the lady
(They have to be shiny)
Two shoes for the giant
(They have to be **leather**)
How many shoes
Do we have altogether?

# Cockatoo Counting

One cockatoo meets one cockatoo.

Pleased to meet you. How d'you do?

Down fly another pair, that's two more.

Two cockatoos plus two make four.

# When Octopuses Cuddle

When octopuses cuddle
They get into a huddle,
Counting all those tentacles
Can get you in a muddle.

# Supper Time

This little pig laid the table,

This little pig stirred the pot,

This little pig laid the fire,

This little pig made it hot.

This little pig cried "Wee wee! Stew for tea!"

And ate the lot!

## I Wish I was a Centipede

I wish I was a centipede.

I'd *wriggle* under roots,

And spend each evening polishing

My hundred muddy boots.

I'd build myself a little home

Beneath the mossy rocks

And spend each morning washing out

My hundred smelly socks.

# There was an Old Woman

There was an old woman who lived in a welly.

The boot was Size One. Much too small, and quite smelly.

She saved up her money and moved to a shoe.

The shoe was much cleaner and bigger (Size Two).

In time, she retired to a sandal (Size Three).

It was airy and light, with a view of the sea.

She's living there still, in the warm summer sun,

And never went back to the welly (Size One).

# Weigh Too Heavy

Elephants are really big
And so are killer whales.
If you tried to weigh them,
You'd surely break the scales.

# Ghostly Counting

One, two, I can go *BOO!*

Three, four, walk through the door,

Five, six, play *scaaary* tricks,

Seven, eight, haunting is great,

Nine, ten, let's do it again!

*BOOooo!*

# Miss One, Two and Three

Miss One, Two and Three
Could never agree
On what kind of buns
They should have for their tea.
Miss One preferred currants,
Miss Two preferred plain,
Miss Three ate the lot
And was sick on the train.

# The Clock Struck One

The clock struck one. The mouse ran down.

Whatever did he do?

He took an hour to climb back up,

And then the clock struck two!

All day the mouse ran up and down.

He thought, enough of that!

He lasted until midnight

Then he moved in with the cat.

# Five Little Snowmen

Five little snowmen
Fishing in the loch,
One caught a cart wheel,
One caught a clock,
One caught a casket
Filled with gold.
One caught a coffee pot
And one caught a cold!

# How Doth the Little Alligator

How doth the little alligator

Take away and add?

He's bought himself a calculator.

Clever little lad!

# The Bears' Phone Call

345 6789?

Goldilocks is on the line!

She's ringing us from Norwich!

She says she's out of porridge!

Out of porridge? Is it true?

Whatever will the poor girl do?

We'll have to send some in the post.

'Til then, she must make do with toast.